Painted eggs

DATE DUE

DEMCO 38-296

Painted eggs

Using dyes, watercolours, gouache, pencil and inks

Heidi Haupt-Battaglia

SEARCH PRESS

First published in Great Britain 1991
Search Press Limited
Wellwood, North Farm Road
Tunbridge Wells, Kent TN2 3DR

Reprinted 1993

Copyright © 1984 by Paul Haupt, Berne

PUBLISHERS' NOTE
There is reference to ''sable'' hair and other animal hair
brushes in this book. It is the Publishers' custom to
recommend synthetic materials as substitutes for animal
products wherever possible. There are now a large
number of brushes available made of artificial fibres and
they are just as satisfactory as those made of natural
fibres.

ISBN 0 85532 672 7 (Pb)
ISBN 0 85532 707 3 (Hb)

Phototypeset by Scribe Design,
123 Watling Street, Gillingham, Kent

Printed in Singapore

Contents

Introduction

The inspiration for egg collecting and, consequently for this book came from what was, in retrospect, a profitable injury. Due to an annoying pain in my right shoulder, I was forced to be totally inactive for weeks on end. I interpreted this to mean that I could make light wrist movements! At that time, Easter was on the horizon, and I set about painting eggs for our celebration. As time was of no consequence then, my first egg was more beautiful than any I had painted before. As I placed each painted egg, one by one, into a basket and saw it filling up, I became obsessed with egg decorating. I alternated between paintbrush and pen, water colours and beads, beeswax and engraving knife and as Easter came and went, and my injury healed, I found I had acquired a whole new outlook on arts and crafts.

We all live in a world of concrete and plastic, noise and bustle, and in the midst of all this we need to build for ourselves a little island of peace and joy – and joy comes from one's work and creative ability. There are many crafts which one can pursue but often these activities come into fashion, stay for a while and then lose their popularity again but, quite by chance, I had found the one which was to fill my life.

As well as painting my own designs, I began to collect eggs by many different artists. In the end, I had so many fine examples of eggs from far and wide that my collection grew to over 1200. A local shop-owner, who handled decorated eggs from many countries, saw my collection and asked if she could use some of them for display purposes and as an inspiration to her customers. My eggs were also subsequently exhibited on two other occasions and then I began to set myself other objectives. My entire circle of friends knew of my passion for decorating eggs, but I wanted to inspire a wider appreciation of this fascinating art form, not just collecting, which can be an interesting hobby, but from a designing point of view. I do not know how many people I have eventually persuaded to tackle egg decorating simply because they watched me at work, but if you do not have any previous experience, you do need a certain amount of guidance.

This is when the germ of an idea for a book

began to form. I did not want to write an educational book covering the decorating techniques which may already have been perfected by skilled craftsmen and women, but one which would give a complete beginner information on the basic techniques needed and such simple details as the suitable types of eggs to use and how to store them when you had completed them. In fact, what I visualised was the type of book I would have purchased when I first began to experiment.

At about the same time, it occurred to me that what would really promote an interest in this fascinating pastime would be an Egg Market at Easter within the walls of my beautiful home town of Berne. Everywhere I went with this request, I was received with full approval: the artists elected an enthusiastic town president and a 'committee for Berne', which offered not only protection to the participants but also real assistance. In addition, crowds of useful helpers volunteered their services.

More than thirty craftsmen and women from Switzerland and Germany eventually spent three days decorating eggs, during which time they were watched by admiring crowds, answered questions, gave advice and even disclosed their secrets; in fact, a school for diverse decorating techniques. Its success was so overwhelming that the 'Bernese Easter Egg Market' was repeated the next year, was improved and then became a firm commitment.

Next Easter will be the eighth market we have held. Now we have seventy craftsmen and women from five different countries who participate. What began in Berne, happily found imitators far and wide. In Switzerland, alone, in 1983, there were ten markets. But the fever did not stop at frontiers between countries and the combined Easter Egg market of the West German Republic and the Netherlands became a fixed institution. Each market has its own individual atmosphere and its unmistakeable aura.

Nowadays, thanks to the enormous interest which has been aroused by what was originally a traditional Easter, or festive occupation, more and more people are becoming involved in designing, not just collecting all-year round examples of this delicate art. If you are a complete novice, I hope that this book will inspire you to experiment with your own designs, and if you are already a converted devotee, I hope you will find new techniques to explore.

All about eggs

Before beginning to paint, carefully consider the type of egg to purchase, the best local source of supply and the necessary preparation. It is important to stress at this stage that only the eggs from domestic fowls should be used. Many species of wild birds are now protected by law and their eggs should never be procured for this purpose.

Buying eggs

The best possible source of supply is from a farm with free-range hens. The eggs are freshly laid and checked before sale. If you explain the purpose for which the eggs are required, the supplier will probably allow you to pick out your own eggs. Eggs from old hens are not really suitable, as they usually have a large number of chalk knots on the surface. If you are fortunate enough to have a farmer as a supplier, ask him if you can have the eggs soiled, as they come out of the hen house. In this way you will not run the risk of buying eggs which have been cleaned with a copper cloth and which are unsuitable for painting.

The egg should:
– Have a regular shape
– Show no indentations, grooves, knots, or thin spots, which look as if they are water-marked
– Have a white shell if required for engraving
   Store the eggs in the refrigerator in a box kept for the purpose. The day before you wish to decorate them, take them out and leave the box of eggs in the warmth of the kitchen.

Washing the eggs

Before painting, the eggs should be gently washed by hand in warm water, to which some detergent has been added. Do not attempt to remove particles of dirt with your finger-nails and do not wear any rings, or you may leave scratch marks on the shells. Never use a scouring cloth as too much vigorous rubbing destroys the imperceptible protective film which covers the shell, with the result that the paint will not be evenly absorbed.

Dry the eggs carefully with a white absorbent teacloth. After washing, do not handle the eggs with greasy hands, as grease spots will repel the paint.

Blowing the eggs

Only the shell of the egg will be decorated and the inside must first be blown out. Four tools are needed:-
– A strong hat-pin, twice as long as an ordinary pin
– A No 3 cross-cleft screwdriver
– A knitting needle, not too thick
– An injection syringe
   Holding the egg tightly with the non-working hand, make a small hole at the very top with the pin. Put the point of the screwdriver into the pin-hole and with one or two careful twists, bore a neat round hole in the shell. Do the same at the other end of the egg. With the knitting needle, thoroughly stir the inside of the egg then with your mouth over one of the holes, blow the contents out of the other hole. Fill the egg with warm water, shake well and blow out again. Repeat this process as often as necessary, until the water that is blown out is completely clear. It is best to keep a constant supply of blown eggs stored in a dry place, ready for use.

The eggs should now be carefully dried and put to stand on a draining rack, with one hole of each against the bottom, and over which an absorbent cloth has been spread. This removes the very last drops of water. Now leave the

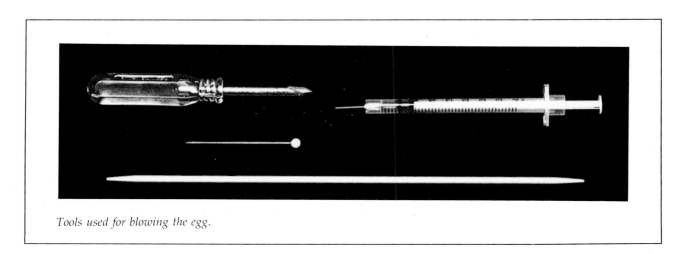

Tools used for blowing the egg.

eggs for two or three days to dry out completely in a dry atmosphere.

If you intend to make this your special craft, there are other ways to overcome the rather tedious and unappetising task of blowing out the eggs by mouth. One alternative is to ask a plumber to fit a special vacuum implement to one of your water taps. A simpler method is to use an injection syringe with a plunger. Make a pin-hole at the pointed end of the egg and a bored hole at the flat end. After the contents have been stirred with the knitting needle, air is pumped through the small pin-hole with the syringe. When the egg is empty, it is cleaned with water as for the blowing by mouth method.

Not every egg is suitable and those with grooves, knots, water marks and distorted shapes should be rejected.

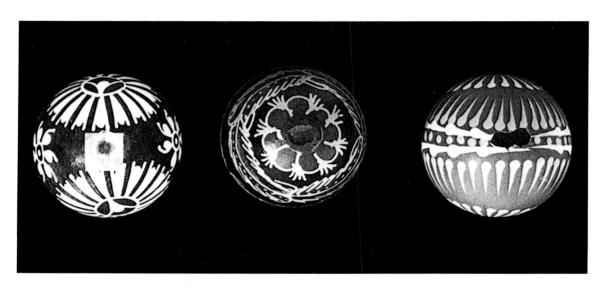

These attractive batik designs are ruined by badly blown holes.

It is vital to emphasise the importance of the correct piercing of the eggs, as well as the thorough washing out of the interior. In the batik eggs from Czechoslavakia, shown above, almost without exception the holes in them have been carelessly pierced, with the openings too large and even chipped in many places. With the least pressure the shells will split even more. Some egg painters try to disguise the fault by smearing wax of the same colour on to the afflicted spot, others glue a little piece of paper over it. For collectors, however, eggs like these are a disgrace and it follows that anyone who breaks an egg so carelessly must also neglect the blowing out process.

Then there is the problem of storing damaged and badly blown eggs! If they are left indoors they disintegrate in time and a horrible smell will emanate from the drawer or cupboard in which they are stored. Even worse; if they are put in a very dry place the residue inside the eggs does not rot at all but dries out, giving the impression at first glance that they have been saved. But, later, you may discover tiny pinpricks criss-crossing the surface, as the inhabitants which have taken up residence busy themselves with your eggs. If you trace these lines, you will see that they come from one of the splintered holes. These minute creatures, which multiply in their thousands if left alone for a while, are mites which feed on the dried egg store. When their favourite food, the dried egg, is all gone they will even nibble the shell and, eventually, destroy the decoration. Mites in a collection of eggs are as damaging as rust in a weapons collection!

11

Eggs painted with drawing ink or watercolours

Before applying the decoration, saturate a cotton wool pad with lemon juice, vinegar or a rinsing agent. Use this to clean the surface of the egg, so removing any last grease spots.

Eggs which are engraved

It is sometimes recommended that instead of blowing the egg, it is boiled for an hour with the contents still inside. This method, however, can pose problems for the collector in the long run:-

1) Albumen and egg yolk may remain, in some places, on the inside of the shell and this makes the egg list to one side. If you are fortunate, the actual engraving will be done exactly opposite this sticky spot! However, this is seldom the case and even the most beautiful egg becomes a source of annoyance if it persistently turns on to one side.

2) The contents of the egg lie, at random, within the shell. This state comes about mostly by chilling with cold water after boiling the egg. They eventually shrink and dry out in the course of a few years, (depending on the porousness of the shell), to a spherical shape as hard as glass which, by very gentle movements of the egg can be transferred wherever one wishes. The danger here is that unreliable visitors who want to examine the egg from all sides are often alarmed by the little gremlin which appears to be inside the shell and shake the egg to check whether anything did actually move, or drop it in their agitation!

3) A chicken egg, as is well known, also contains a certain amount of fat. Quite often, this fat seeps through the pores on to the surface area, but only after years have passed. An artistically decorated egg is only half as attractive to us if it is greasy to the touch and, occasionally, this greasy film even impairs the paint on the egg.

In order to overcome all these disadvantages, it is better to blow out the eggs to be engraved beforehand. They are, after all, no more fragile in this condition than boiled eggs!

The dried contents of a boiled egg become as hard as glass marble with the passage of time.

Eggs for batik technique

The greatest masters of this wax-relief technique are the Huzules, a people who come from Ukrania. They do not blow out the eggs first but work on them in their raw state. If necessary, they wash them first in about a quarter of a litre (½ pint) of warm water, to which a tablespoonful of vinegar has been added.

A full egg, raw or boiled, sinks when it is immersed in the dye mixture and absorbs the cold batik dye very evenly. A blown out egg is lighter and therefore floats on the surface, so it must also be filled with liquid dye, using a syringe.

To sum up:-
1) Raw eggs are easily covered with dye. The blowing out process is laborious, however, as the egg is emptied after the work has been completed. The spot where the lips touch the egg must be covered with sticky tape. Also, the durability of the egg is doubtful.
2) There are difficulties in plunging blown out eggs into the liquid. The advantage of this method is that it ensures maximum durability.
3) Boiled eggs are easily covered with the dye but problems will be experienced with preservation.

For collecting purposes, it is therefore better to use blown out eggs.

Eggs for all other techniques

Wash them as described on page 8.

Background colouring

Many species of birds use colourful patterns on their eggs to disguise them in the nest and these can sometimes serve as a suitable background for painting. For example:-
– White as a background for silhouette shapes
– All shades of beige, from egg-shell white through to caramel can be used as a background for Indian ink drawings
– Many species of ducks lay eggs with shells as fine as silk and of a distinct green shade, which can serve as a delicate background for watercolours, or pen and ink drawings
– The freckles on turkey eggs can be used as a background for small white motifs
– The well-proportioned little brown flecks on guinea-fowl eggs look particularly attractive behind strong coloured motifs

If other background colours are required, however, you will need to use natural or synthetic dyes. There is a considerable choice available from most art or craft shops.

Colouring the eggs

You can either use natural materials, such as onion skins, as a source of dye for colouring the eggs, textiles which already contain strong dyes, or chemical colours available from most craft shops, or chemists.

Dyeing with natural colours

The colours obtained from natural sources are softer than those achieved with chemical dyes and the results are always unpredictable.
Sources of dye:-
- Pale onion peel; boiled for 1 hour gives brick red through to dark brown
- Red onion peel; rusty red
- Redwood (from chemist); wine red
- Logwood (from chemist); when fresh the colour is violet to aubergine, after a week or two it fades to coffee brown
- Tagetes flower; this genus of plants have yellow or orange flowers and give shades of sulphur and mustard yellow
- Tansy; numerous plants having yellow flowers in flat-topped clusters which produce French bean green
- Walnut tree leaves; shades of olive green to brown
- Cochineal (from chemist); cyclamen red
- Sandalwood (from chemist); golden yellow
- Coffee infusion; light brown
- Tea infusion; dark beige

Each boiled dye creates its own shade and will vary from batch to batch. You can obtain other colours by mixing the dyes.

Equipment and materials required
Tablespoon wrapped in nylon tights, or a wooden spoon
1 enamel saucepan
Cotton cloths
Natural dye or stain
2 litres (3½ pints) water for 8 to 10 eggs

Tablespoonful of wood ash to each litre (1¾ pints) of water
Sheet of white paper

Method
The peel of a boiled onion can supply shades of brick red through to rust red and the colours obtained from redwood and logwood can range from wine red through to coffee brown. The list above gives a selection of colours suitable for most requirements.

Once the shells have been dyed, they need to be treated with a mordant to fix the colours. You can use a chemical medium, such as alum, but the best results are obtained with natural wood ash. To obtain this, clean out any charcoal from a barbeque tray, then light a wood fire. When this has cooled, rake out the ashes and store them in a plastic bag.

Put the water sufficient for 8 to 10 eggs into the saucepan, adjusting this amount for more or fewer eggs. Add a handful of the natural dye material, noting that cochineal needs only a small coffee spoonful. Boil vigorously for quarter of an hour, then test the density of the dye on the piece of white paper. Depending on the result of this test and the colour you wish to achieve, either add more dye material or more water.

Now strain into the mixture a heaped tablespoonful of wood ash to each litre (1¾ pints) of water. It is surprising what this unattractive mordant can do, as the colour of the dye is noticeably intensified! The mixture must now be carefully sieved, otherwise dye material or particles of wood ash may cling to the eggshell and prevent even dyeing.

Using a tablespoon wrapped in nylon tights, or a wooden spoon to avoid scratching the shell, plunge the egg, which must first be filled with water, into the dye mixture and boil as

Natural dyes, from left to right, pale onion skin, red onion skin, redwood, fresh logwood, logwood after two months, walnut leaves, tagetes and tansy.

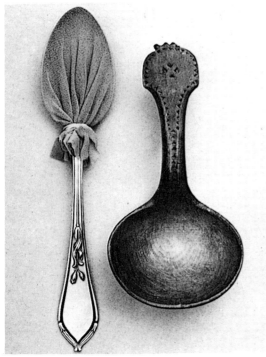

To avoid scratching the coloured shell, take the eggs out of the dye with a wooden spoon or a metal one wrapped in nylon.

15

Only the front of an egg dyed with textiles is attractive.

From left to right, the first five eggs are dyed with pale and dark cochineal, sandalwood, tea and coffee. The last two are dyed with textiles.

long as is necessary to obtain the required shade of colour. It is quite normal, when eight to ten eggs are plunged into the same mixture, for all of them to show a slight difference in intensity of colour. Each egg varies, depending on the food ingested by the chicken or fowl which lays it, and no one eggshell is exactly like another.

When you are satisfied with the colour, scoop the eggs out of the liquid and rinse them immediately under cold running water. Let the water run over the egg then, if necessary, rub away any impurities very carefully with your thumbs. Dry the eggs with a clean absorbent teacloth and set them aside until they are completely dried out.

Dyeing with textiles

Surprising effects can be achieved by covering raw, white eggs with material from something no longer in use, such as a tie with a small pattern. This means that the finished eggs will not be as durable as blown eggs.

Equipment and materials
Tablespoon wrapped in nylon tights, or a wooden spoon
1 enamel saucepan
Cotton cloths
1 litre (1¾ pints) water for 8 to 10 eggs
Raw, white chicken eggs
Suitable fabric printed with a small design but not too highly coloured
Length of thread or twine

Method
The pattern chosen must be small enough to be spread over the facing side of the egg, whilst forming a ridged effect on the back of the egg through the folds of the material.

Tighten the fabric evenly over the curve of the egg, smoothing out as many creases as possible over the front surface, then tie it together with thread at the back of the egg and trim away any excess material. Once the egg has been wrapped in this way, barely cover it with cold water and boil gently for one hour, then unwrap the fabric and gently shake the egg until it is dry. The fabric can only be used once for this purpose, so each egg is a one-off original.

Dyeing with chemical colours

It is much easier to use synthetic dyes rather than natural dyes but you will never be able to produce the same soft, shaded colours. Their great advantage over other types of dye is that they are colour-fast.

First mix sufficient quantity of dye to cover the number of eggs required as given on the tube or packet. The eggs to be dyed are then blown out, filled with water and lowered into the dye mixture. You will be delighted with the bright red, royal blue, radiant yellow and rich violet colours you can obtain with synthetic dyes, which can also be mixed to produce secondary colours, for example, yellow and blue to give shades of green.

Equipment and materials
Tablespoon wrapped in nylon tights, or a wooden spoon
1 enamel saucepan
Cotton cloths
2 litres (3½ pints) water for 8 to 10 eggs
Artificial dyes, noting that the most common are dye blocks, batik dye and fabric dyes, available from the chemist
Mordant
Sheet of white paper

Method
As soon as the eggs are removed from the dye, work as given for dyeing with natural colours.

Collecting and caring for painted eggs

It is quite amazing how a collection of eggs is soon established and what started out as an artistic experiment becomes an obsession! One egg here and another there, (those which turned out so well we just have to keep them), a couple of wonderful examples from a like-minded friend, or just your child's first attempt at painting eggs and, suddenly, you are a collector.

To begin with you may place the delicate miniatures in a display case, hang them up or just leave them nonchalantly lying around on top of a chest of drawers to invite comment! Their increasing numbers eventually lead you to stow them in a shallow basket but when that is also full to overflowing, you realise that you have something of a problem on your hands. They need to be exhibited to their best effect, where harsh light will not fade or damage them and kept well away from dirty and clumsy hands. This is when you need the advice of an expert!

Arranging

The best way to arrange and display the eggs is to embed them in suitable grain, pointed end to the top. Handle them very gently but make sure they are secure and will not move. In the first few months, it is recommended that you turn over the grain occasionally with your finger, to ensure that tiny mites have not infested it.

You can purchase special strong cardboard boxes about 24 × 34 cm (9½ × 13½ in) which have 6 air holes, each of about 2 cm (¾ in) diameter, punched into the sides of the box about a third of the way down. Fill the box with grain to a depth of about 2 cm (¾ in).

Suitable grains

Seed for exotic birds; beige and speckled
Rape seed, a fodder plant; dark brown
Poppy seed; greyish-blue
Red millet; rusty red
Raw rice; sand-coloured
Bleached rice; ivory
Seed for wild birds; mottled
Millett; ivory
Lentils; olive green
Peas, dried; yellow or green
Soya beans; green

Unsuitable grains

Legumes larger than peas
Fine ground meal; could block blow holes
Birdsand; too harsh, may damage paint
Barley; floury film clings to the eggs

Storing

Arrange the eggs in the grain to give a pleasing display, see opposite. You should decide how you wish to present them as a collection, say, either according to the technique used, or the country of origin, or a particular artist. Store the boxes in a dry, dark cupboard, away from too much heat.

When each box is completed, write out a list of the contents, numbering each egg and giving details of the type of egg, the technique used, the name of the artist, the date and any other details which will help you to remember the pleasure you have experienced in assembling the collection.

Template designs

This is a delightfully simple and natural way to decorate eggs which are intended for immediate consumption. Children will especially enjoy experimenting with this method.

Natural templates

With this method you are using a natural template, such as a leaf, to block out the background dye.

Eggs

Raw, smooth chicken eggs, pierced with a fine pin at both ends.

Equipment and materials

Pins
Scissors
Suitable flowers and foliage
Piece of nylon stocking
Thread or fine string
Natural or synthetic dyes
Bacon rind

Method

Select and pick well-shaped flowers and pieces of foliage and leave them to dry of their own accord.

Spread the flower or foliage carefully over the curve on the front of the egg and hold it in place with pins. Moisten the egg with water. Now place the nylon fabric evenly over the centre of the plant and right round to the back of the egg, removing the pins as you go, pull it together at the back and secure with thread.

For natural dyes, into a saucepan put 2 litres (3½ pints) of cold water and 2 handfuls of either onion peel, redwood or logwood, see page 14. Place the eggs in the water in a single layer and boil for as long as required. For synthetic dyes, make up the dye as given in the instructions.

Cut away the fabric with scissors and remove the plant template. If you wish, polish the eggs with bacon rind first and then put them into cold water to chill, or just chill them at once.

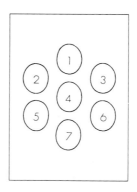

Template designs, opposite.
All eggs by Heidi Haupt.
1. Ground, pale onion skin; motif chervil.
2. Ground, redwood; motif figwort.
3. Ground, coffee; motif fern leaf.
4. Ground, red onion skin; motif lady's smock.
5. Ground, tea; motif columbine.
6. Ground, sandalwood; motif wood sorrel.
7. Ground, pale onion skin; motif hairy vetch.

Engraved designs

There is really no more rewarding way of decorating an egg than by engraving. It offers a whole range of advantages over other egg decorating techniques, as follows:-

1) Few tools are necessary.

2) Once you have learnt to manipulate the knife adeptly, you have already mastered the art of engraving.

3) No matter how often the work is interrupted it is always possible to continue from the point of interruption, and the fresh start will be imperceptible.

4) You do not need to set aside a whole Saturday afternoon or an evening's leisure in order to complete one egg, as it can be continued over a period of time.

5) You can choose the best light source by which to work, without being restricted to a table laden with saucepans, shells and a wide variety of other equipment.

6) Engraved eggs are destined for eternity,

Engraved designs, opposite.

1. Ground, redwood. *Johanna Huber.*
2. Ground, coffee. *Johanna Huber.*
3. Ground, red onion skin. *Johanna Huber.*
4. Ground, chemical dye, grey-black. *Johanna Huber.*
5–7. Ground, chemical dyes violet, blue and brown. *Marie Reusser.*
8. Ground, red onion skin. *Marie Reusser.*
9,10. Ground, walnut leaves. *Vreni Messmer.*
11,12. Ground, oilpaints, purple, violet. *Beate Frauenfelder.*

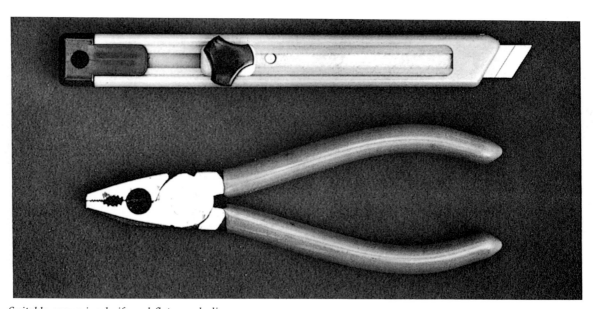

Suitable engraving knife and flat-nosed pliers.

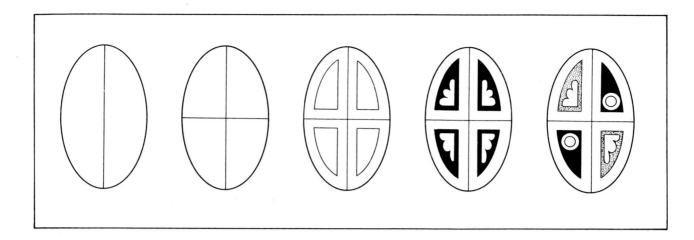

because where dyes may fade, indelible engraved designs remain constant. I know of engraved eggs which are 50, or even 70 years old, and they have lost nothing of their beauty.

7) Provided you keep a knife and flat-nosed pliers in your luggage and a couple of dyed eggs in a protective cardboard box, no rainy day away from home will be wasted.

8) Engraving is a wonderful medium for people employed in professions where a certain amount of time is spent waiting, such as nurses, or for patients whiling away time in a waiting room, and for lovers just waiting with impatience. Every free minute can be fully utilised!

Engraved eggs

It is important to choose a design which will lend itself to this medium and will also enhance the contours of the egg.

Eggs

These should be blown out and dyed, preferably with a dark dye. Batik dyes harden the eggshells and the engraving has to be done more firmly than on eggs shaded with natural dyes.

Equipment and materials

Pencil, sharp but not too soft
India rubber
Small flat-nosed pliers
Strong knife, consisting of plastic and metal
Final coat of lacquer

Note: The knife should have a notched blade which can be pushed, by means of thumb pressure of the right hand, over one stage at a time up to the required length. It is easier to use if the blade is pushed out a little more than one notch. If the tip is no longer sharp enough, the blade can be shortened one notch, by using the flat-nosed pliers. Instead of a paper knife, another sharp tool may be used, for example, a scalpel, a cut-throat razor, a nail, an awl, or a sharpened sewing-machine needle attached to a fixing pencil.

Method

The more evenly the egg has been dyed, the more beautiful the end product will be. You should only partially mark out the pattern with a pencil, otherwise you may smudge some of the outlines as you handle the egg. The motif needs to be sketched over the whole egg a bit at a time, and as each section is completed, go over the pencil marks with the paper knife. You will only need a very fine scratch to define the outline.

24

Engraved designs, *above.*
All eggs by Heidi Haupt.

    1. Ground, logwood.
    2. Ground, chemical dye, damson blue.
    3. Ground, plum tree bark, vermillion.
    4. Ground, logwood.
    5. Ground, chemical dye, violet.
    6. Ground, chemical dye, slate-blue.
  7,8. Ground, chemical dye, royal blue.
9–12. Ground, chemical dye, dark blue.

If it your first experiment with engraving, you will probably find it easier to begin in the following manner:-

1) Draw a straight line with a pencil from one end of the egg to the other. This is much easier than you think and it follows the biggest curve of the egg. Mark a fine line with the knife over this pencil line, only moving forward about 2 cm (¾ in) at a time, and then gently scratch back again. The noise that is produced should just be a gentle scraping sound, not like the squealing of pigs!

Using this action, work each scratch into the previous one, like a train shunting backwards and forwards. In this way you will find that the line is cleaner than if you pull the knife through from the top to the bottom in one movement. If you go back to the beginning of the line again, you will make definite furrows in the line.

2) Mark out the egg into four quarters using a similar movement.

3) Now mark a line round the middle of the egg to create 8 sections.

4) Reduce these 8 areas by means of a border, which is drawn about 6 mm (¼ in) inside the division line.

5) Finally, pencil in a simple motif in each of the 8 sectors and engrave it out cleanly, so that the white of the eggshell shines through. Scratch evenly in all directions, but carefully follow the division lines. If you want to let your imagination run riot you could alternate between 2 different motifs.

6) If you have 3 shades of dye visible on your egg, only engrave on relatively small defined areas, so that the colour itself is heightened.

7) When you first begin engraving, in your enthusiasm you may push the point of the knife blade further than is necessary into the shell. That, in fact, is how you learn what sort of pressure the eggshell is able to withstand!

8) Engraved eggs require no special after-treatment. However, if it happens that large, white areas were initially scratched out and these become unstable as the work progresses, you will need to varnish the egg to preserve it.

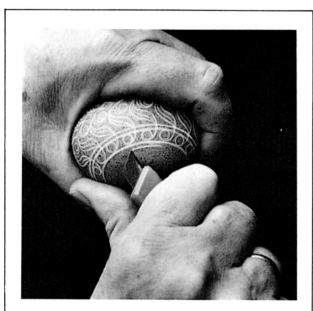

Gently scratch the shell with the top of the blade.

Scratch out lines and areas.

A selection of motifs which can be used for an eight-section egg. Use stylized, not realistic motifs.

27

Drawn designs

The surface of an eggshell provides an excellent background for a freehand design, drawn either with a lead pencil, coloured pencils, or pen and ink. Crayons are also suitable but the chalk type will easily rub off and it is better to use wax crayons.

Lead pencil designs

The motifs shown opposite have all been sketched in with an ordinary pencil.

Eggs

These should be blown out, see page 8.

Equipment and materials

Sharp, hard pencil
India rubber
Matt or gloss varnish

Method

If the drawing is to be taken right round the egg, once the front is completed it should be varnished and allowed to dry before continuing with the drawing on the back of the egg. This will avoid any possibility of smudging the drawing, when no amount of rubbing out will help.

Coloured pencil designs

Eggs

These should be blown out, see page 8, and either left their natural colour or dyed.

Equipment and materials

A variety of coloured pencils
Matt or gloss varnish

Method

Hold the egg in the palm of the hand in order to support it firmly, as the pencils only give sufficient colour if applied with a strong pressure. When the drawing is completed, protect it with varnish.

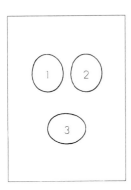

Lead pencil drawings.
(*Suitable for large eggs, such as a goose egg*).
1. Natural colour, white. *Alfred Hofkunst.*
2. Natural colour, white. *Gottfried Erfurth.*
3. Natural colour, greenish-grey. *Heidi Haupt.*

Crayon designs

Eggs
Hard-boiled, suitable for eating. Blown out eggs are unsuitable for this medium, as strong pressure is needed to apply the crayons.

Equipment and materials
Sharpened wax crayons, which have been softened over a lighted candle
Matt or gloss varnish

Method
The drawing on the front must be varnished and allowed to dry, before completing the back.

Felt-tipped pen designs
Felt-tipped pens are a splendid drawing medium, being easy to handle and available in a range of rich, bright colours. Not all of them are colour-fast, however, so do make sure that you obtain permanent colours which are quickly absorbed into the eggshell and will not fade.

Eggs
These can either be blown out or hard-boiled, ready to eat, with natural or dyed backgrounds.

Equipment and materials
Felt-tipped pens in a variety of colours

Method
No initial pencil sketch is required as this cannot be erased afterwards. Use the pens to draw the design but do not work on too large an area at once. Do a small section at a time and allow this to dry thoroughly before continuing with the next area.

Tip
Many felt-tipped pens, particularly those of inferior quality, have one undesirable tendency: the colours run and smudge easily, either spoiling the design as it is being worked, or subsequently. Always test them on a spare or broken shell before beginning your design.

Pen and ink designs
The examples shown opposite and on the following pages have all been drawn with a pen and Indian ink. Pen and ink drawings are particularly attractive when specific areas are coloured in before varnishing the egg.

Eggs
These should be blown out, see page 8. Use either white chicken and goose eggs, brown and beige chicken eggs, greenish duck eggs, or those where the background has been delicately tinted with natural or synthetic dyes.

Equipment and materials
Fine ink pens, which only draw upward strokes *or*
Sable brushes Nos 000 and 00
Fine, hard pencil
India rubber
Indian ink
Gloss varnish

Method
Remove any grease from the eggshell with vinegar, lemon juice or detergent. This will stop the ink application running into an indefinable line, or breaking up into thin droplets of colour.

Sketch in the design with a pencil at first, then with a pen, or brush and ink. Remember to erase any pencil marks which still show with a soft rubber.

Apply a final coat of varnish as a protection.

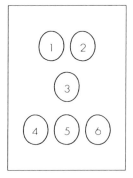

Crayon drawings, *see page 32.*
All eggs by Heidi Haupt.

1. Ground, natural, white; red and black design.
2. Ground, cochineal; black and white design.

Red pencil drawing.

3. Ground, natural, white; red design.

Coloured pencil drawings.

4. Ground, chemical dye, light blue; multi-coloured design.
5. Ground, chemical dye, light green; multi-coloured design.
6. Ground, natural, light brown; multi-coloured drawing.

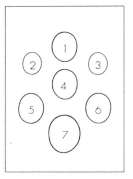

Indian ink drawings, *see page 34.*
All eggs by Christine Schneider.

1. Ground, natural, white; background for motif, dispersion dye, violet.
2. Ground, natural, light brown; motif, head and legs white poster paint, halo, gold poster paint.
3. Ground, natural, white.
4. Ground, cream, duck egg; motif, cockscomb red poster paint.
5. Ground, natural, white; background and various decorations, gold poster paint.
6. Ground, natural, white; background for motif, violet poster paint.
7. Ground, white, goose egg.

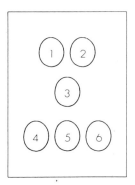

Felt pen drawings, *see page 33.*

1,2. Brown, white and black. *Erwin Daepp.*
3. Multi-coloured. *Christoph Schelbert.*
4–6. Left to right, blue/white, red/black, white/brown. *Madeleine Meier.*

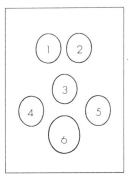

Indian ink drawings, *see page 35.*
All eggs by Heidi Haupt.

1,2. Hen's egg. Ground, walnut leaves; design shades of olive green.
3. Hen's egg. Ground, tagetes.
4. Hen's egg. Ground, cochineal, light pink.
5. Duck egg. Ground, natural, absinthe green.
6. Goose egg. Ground, natural, white.

Etched designs

With most decorating techniques, colour is applied to a background in one way or another, but a similar effect can be achieved by removing colour from the background. With this etching method, certain parts of the basic colour are eaten away when acid is applied. This method of decorating eggs is very popular in Switzerland.

Etching

The colour effects achieved with this method are very delicate and muted.

Eggs

These should be blown out, see page 8, or hard-boiled, ready to eat. Dye the eggshell, preferably with a natural dye, in a colour which is not too dark, or the acid corrosion will scarcely be visible.

Equipment and materials

Sharp, wooden toothpicks squeezed into a pencil holder, or metal nib pushed into a pen holder
Cotton cloth
Lemon juice or citrate of lemon powder diluted with a little water
Vinegar
Absorbent cloth
Blotting paper

Method

You work with these acids in exactly the same way as you would with ink. The only difference is that a stroke with acid takes away the colour instead of applying it, as with ink.

Only allow a few strokes to run into each other, or you will lose sight of the final effect. Use an absorbent cloth to dab away the acid at the right time, usually a couple of seconds after the application but this will obviously be affected by the concentration of the acid. If a drop of acid remains on the egg, soak up this surplus amount with the corner of a piece of blotting paper, before dabbing it with the absorbent cloth. An acid spot which is not dealt with immediately can spread and spoil the whole design.

Tip

Citric acid and other weak acids recommended here will fade quickly. These concentrations are particularly suitable for decorating eggs which are intended for consumption.

When an egg is intended for collection purposes, domestic bleach, suitably diluted, may be used but care must be taken in handling this and it must be kept out of reach of children.

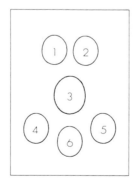

Etched designs, *opposite*.

1,2. Ground, red onion skin; motif citric acid. *Heidi Haupt.*
  3. Ground, chemical dye, greyish brown; motif domestic bleach. *Madeleine Meier.*
  4. Ground, redwood; motif domestic bleach. *Madeleine Meier.*
  5. Ground, logwood; motif domestic bleach. *Madeleine Meier.*
  6. Ground, chemical dye, brown; motif domestic bleach. *Madeleine Meier.*

Painted designs

The type of paint you wish to use will obviously affect the choice of design. The delicacy of the watercolour medium needs a softly shaded background and a design drawn from nature, while poster paints call for stronger colours and a bold motif.

Painting with watercolours

It is much easier to paint with watercolours on paper than on eggs! The tendency is to put far too much water on the egg so that drops of colour roll all over the slippery surface of the egg.

Eggs

These should be blown out, white or primed hen, goose and duck eggs, or eggs dyed with natural or synthetic dyes. Prepare the eggs as given on page 8.

Equipment and materials

A fine, hard pencil
Sable paintbrushes Nos 000, 1 and 6
Knitting needle
Gloss or satin varnish; you can use colourless nail varnish for gloss finish and an acrylic fixative for a satin effect
A flower pot filled with earth, or a heavy container with a narrow neck
Paper handkerchief for cleaning the paintbrush

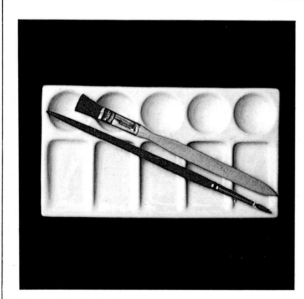

Use the flat brush for the primer and the pointed one for painting. Allow the colours to mix freely in the palette.

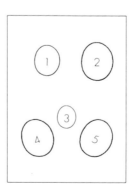

Painting with watercolours, opposite.
1,2. Primed with watercolours.
  3. Bantam egg. *Heidi Haupt.*
  4. Goose egg. *Ursula Jagg.*
  5. Goose egg. *Gertrud Hirsch.*

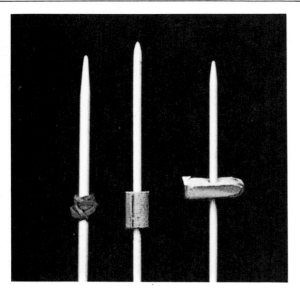

Three ways of holding the egg; knitting needle wrapped with elastic bands; sticking-plaster or a piece of india rubber.

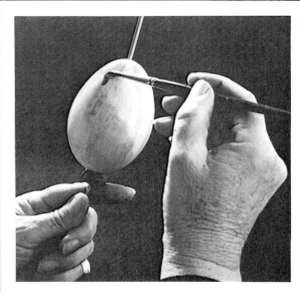

Moisten the egg all over to prime it.

Note: About two-thirds of the way down the knitting needle, fix a small piece of india rubber, several layers of sticky tape, a layer of sticking plaster or several elastic bands wound round each other, to hold the egg in position for painting.

Method

Prepare the egg as given on page 12. Trace out the motif required with a fine, hard pencil. The egg is now ready to be primed, and is placed on the knitting needle.

Holding the knitting needle underneath the restricting device with the left hand, moisten the surface area of the egg with the large brush and dab on a few spots of dye from top to bottom, so that the colours flow downwards into each other. If you then hold the needle at both ends and turn the egg round and round, coloured patterns are produced which can easily be assimilated into the desired motif. Stand the needle in the pot and let the egg dry thoroughly.

To dry the egg, insert the needle into a heavy container.

The motif already drawn underneath the primer can now be painted on and allowed to dry. Finally, coat the finished egg with varnish.

Tips

If the egg looks particularly attractive when it has been primed it may no longer need the motif to be painted on and this can remain as a shadowy image.

You can enhance this faintly visible picture still further where a flower motif has been drawn, by painting in a seemingly naturally planned beetle. The whole effect then looks rather like a photographic close-up.

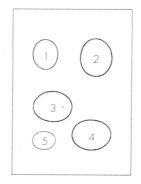

All eggs by Heidi Haupt.
See page 42.
See page 42.
1. Watercolours, peacock egg.
2–4. Watercolours, goose eggs.
5. Watercolours, hen's egg.

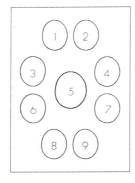

See page 43.
1,2. Watercolours, duck eggs. *Anne-Maria Trechslin.*
2,4. Watercolours, hen's eggs. *Ursula Taggi.*
5. Watercolours, goose egg. *Anne-Maria Trechslin.*
6–9. Watercolours, hen's eggs. *Ursula Taggi.*

See page 44.
1–9. Watercolours, hen's eggs, natural.
Chinese eggs, for special occasions, feel like silk because they are polished with steel wool before painting. The eggs are not blown but sucked out, so only a single small hole is produced.

44

Rings can be made from wooden beads or discs.

Painting with strong colours

Working with bold colours, such as those achieved with tempera, gouache and poster paints, is particularly suitable for painting eggs, because it is easy to apply the rich colours so that the egg is evenly covered. In addition, when these heavier paints are used, decorative relief effects can be produced.

Eggs

These should be natural blown out eggs, or those already primed with Indian ink, or synthetic and natural dyes.

Equipment and materials

A fine, hard pencil
Paper knife as given for engraved eggs
Sable paintbrushes Nos 000 and 0
Ring made of wooden beads about 10 cm (4 in) diameter, with an inside diameter of 3 cm (1½ in)
Gloss or satin varnish

Note: The ring is used to store the egg for the short time it needs to dry. The egg nestles against the ring without any damage being caused to the painting. A ring of this size will fit up to the size of a goose egg.

Method

The design is first traced on to the egg with a pencil and then scratched out gently with the paper knife, as it is easier to guide the paintbrush along the fine indentations made by the knife. Painted eggs which are first engraved in this way always look very professional. If you then add single spots of colour, or small, simple motifs with several rich colours, the egg will almost have the appearance of an example of a goldsmith's relief work.

As the egg has been painted with quick drying colours, it will soon be dry enough to handle. Do remember, however, that the areas where extra layers have been applied will need a little longer before it is safe to handle them. When thoroughly dry, apply the varnish very carefully.

Tip

It is important to apply the varnish to any relief areas of the egg very thoroughly, so that it completely permeates the layers underneath.

45

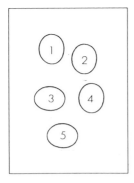

Painting with bold colours, *opposite.*
All eggs by Heidi Haupt.
1–5. Ground, black Indian ink; motifs painted with
poster paint and decorated with white dots.

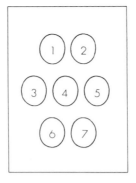

Painting with bold colours, *see page 50.*
All eggs by Doris Epple.
1–5. Ground, natural colours.
6,7. Ground, black poster paint.

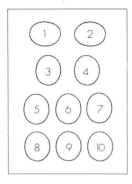

Painting with bold colours, *see page 48.*
All eggs by Heidi Haupt.
Motifs are painted in shades of pure red, orange,
signal red, garnet, raspberry, rusty red and
cyclamen, with added raised white dots.
  1,2. Ground, cochineal.
  3,4. Ground, red mordant.
  5–8. Ground, cochineal.
    9. Ground, redwood.
  10. Ground, cochineal.

Painting with bold colours, added raised white dots,
see page 51.
All eggs by Heidi Haupt.
1–3. Ground, tagetes.
  4. Ground, red onion skin.
  5. Ground, synthetic dye.
  6. Ground, tagetes.
  7. Ground, walnut leaves.
  8. Ground, tagetes.
  9. Ground, tea.

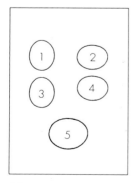

Painting with bold colours, *see page 49.*
All eggs by Heidi Haupt.
1. Ground, natural, cream; motif white poster paint.
2. Ground, black Indian ink omitting motif; motif red
   and gold.
3. Ground, black Indian ink omitting motif.
4. Ground, gold chemical dye.
5. Ground, black Indian ink omitting motif.

Batik designs

In many countries, Easter is the traditional time for painting eggs and one of the most popular techniques is to block out a design with hot wax before dyeing the egg, just as you would with fabric. This method is known as wax relief, or batik.

In Eastern Europe, wives of the farmers in such countries as East Germany, Czechoslavakia, Romania, Hungary and Yugoslavia, all bustle about at this particular time of year with pans of hot wax, bent soup spoons and split goose feathers and pins. The feathers are cut and used to apply the wax and the pins attached to wooden rods, used to produce dotted patterns. The Huzules, a Ukranian race from Romania and Russia with a rich tradition in folklore crafts, also use this batik technique. However, their equipment does not consist of feathers and pins but a special tool made from a wooden rod to one end of which a tiny funnel is fastened by means of copper wire. This tool is called a 'kistkas'. The little container for the wax opens into a very fine pipe, out of which the hot liquid flows on to the egg. The eggs designed by the Huzules can be easily and immediately distinguished from any other decorated by the batik method. Their sketchwork is exceptionally fine and extremely varied, although many favourite decorations and motifs appear again and again. These little works of art are known as 'pisankis'.

Without wishing to dampen your enthusiasm, some of the disadvantages of the batik method should be pointed out. The housewife, who can spare half-an-hour to decorate an egg before preparing a meal, may well be able to reach out for an engraving knife, but it's not that simple if you wish to decorate an egg with batik, as you need to have at least a whole afternoon free to do so. If you wish to explore the tremendous possibilities this technique has to offer, arrangements have to be made for the children to be cared for; someone has to feed the animals and a good friend must be coerced into ironing the washing! Also, many items of equipment are required before you can begin this adventure and must be laid out on a table, which needs to be covered with several layers of newspaper. You will need a little stove and some wax; a bowl of water and several saucepans for the dye; kistkas with fine tubes and kistkas with thick tubes; paper handker-

Painting with bold colours, opposite.
All eggs by Heidi Haupt.

1. Pheasant egg, natural colour; motif crested lark.
2. Turkey egg, natural colour; motif dove engraved on shell and painted iris.
3. Pheasant egg, natural colour; motif woodlark.
4. Hen's egg, pale onion skin ground; motif two butterflies.
5. Hen's egg, chemical dye ground, light grey; motif eagle owl.
6. Hen's egg, pale onion skin ground; motif blackbird.
7. Hen's egg, pale onion skin ground; motif pair of birds.
8. Goose egg, pale onion skin ground; motif duck and duckling.
9. Hen's egg, pale onion skin ground; motif cockerel.

Two batik eggs. The one on the left shows the pisankis method and on the right, the sorbisch method.
Both eggs by Elisabeth Stahli.

chieves; spoons, candles and matches; and so on and so on. . . . .

Once everything is to hand you may think you can begin! The wax is flowing beautifully in the kistkas – but the wax in the pan is beginning to smoke. So you move the pan away, taking care not to spill any wax, and the smoke evaporates. In the meantime, the wax in the kistkas has cooled off and will not flow any more. You manage to overcome these problems and the egg with its first wax application is ready to put into the dye. Beforehand, however, the blown holes have to be blocked with wax, which means you must remember to prevent the lightened egg from rising to the surface. You rush around looking for a suitable tumbler or glass to place over the egg to hold it down. Again, the wax smokes; a corner of the newspaper has caught fire; the egg must be turned over in the dye – and all this can happen in the course of half-an-hour! You may feel that

this catalogue of possible disasters is too graphic, but it is essential to ensure that only someone with plenty of time to spare, a comfortable place in which to work, well-bred children and nerves of steel will attempt this technique.

A distinction is made between the two types of egg batik – those done with goose feathers and those done with a kistkas. The most

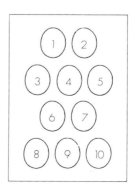

Batik designs, *opposite*.
1,2. Showing old Swiss patterns.
3–10. Showing new Swiss patterns.

54

A blown egg must be prevented from rising to the surface by a heavy object.

The can is filled with sand and the spoon is bent down to the right.

beautiful designs worked with a feather come from the East German area of Lausitz, where a craft-loving people, the Sorben, devote much care and love to egg decorating. In order to differentiate between the two methods, all eggs designed with bird feathers and pins are referred to as 'sorbisch', and all those marked with a kistkas, or pen-nib, as 'pisankis'.

Sorbisch method

This method is probably the easier of the two to work but it does not enable such fine and detailed designs to be produced.

Eggs

These should be blown out, see page 8, and the blow holes blocked with waterproof glue or wax. The egg must be weighted down when it is dipped into the dye mixture and needs to be turned regularly when submerged, so that the dye spreads evenly.

Hard-boiled eggs may be used and these sink in the dye mixture. Raw eggs also sink in the dye mixture but need to be blown out after decorating.

Equipment and materials

A fine pencil
A can, ½ litre (¾ pint) capacity filled with sand
A spoon with the handle bent down to the right
Goose feathers with 5 different cuts
Wooden rod and either a pin with round glass head, or metal head, inserted
Drinking glass
Bowl of cold water
Candle stump, or night light, which is placed 5 cm (2 in) under the spoon as a heater
Wax mixture of half beeswax to guarantee adherence and half stearin to guarantee fluidity
Paper towel or handkerchief
Newspapers
Dye mixture, prepared according to manufacturer's instructions
Absorbent cloth
Final varnish, or bacon rind

Method

With a fine pencil outline the design. Pinch the feather quill between the thumb and index finger, with the thumb uppermost, and plunge

Tools for the sorbisch method include pins with differing large round heads, and split goose feathers.

it tip first into the hot wax, which should not be smoking. Hold the egg and the spoon as near to each other as possible, so that not too much heat is lost on the way from one to the other. Trace over the pencil patterns with the wax impregnated feather very quickly and then pull the feather free to release the fronds. If the feather is left too long on the egg, it will congeal solidly.

Use the round head of the pin to position dots or stripes of wax, but leave the pin in the hot wax to heat before starting, or the wax spots may stick to the eggshell.

Now place the egg into the prepared dye solution. It must be completely covered with dye. Leave it immersed for about half-an-hour, or until it has attained the required density of dye. Turn the egg and move it about in the solution every so often. Remove the egg from the dye and dry with an absorbent cloth.

Hold the egg as close as possible to the heater so that the wax on the pinhead does not cool.

The wax which has been applied is now removed by holding the egg over a candle flame. The melted wax is wiped away with a paper towel or handkerchief. To melt the wax more quickly, heat the oven then turn it off. Hold the egg lightly, away from any wax, and rotate your hand gently in the oven, making sure you do not touch the sides of the oven. Dab away the liquid wax with a paper towel.

If the design consists of more than one colour, the wax application must be repeated on a different section of the egg for each colour. Begin with the brightest colour first and work through the cycle to the darkest, eg, bright yellow, dark yellow, orange, red and then black.

Eggs intended for consumption can be given a final polish with bacon rind. This is not suitable for an egg which is intended for a collection, however, and the egg should be varnished with lacquer for a more intensive lustre.

Pisankis method

Very fine detail can be achieved with this type of batik but you need a steady hand!

Eggs

As given for the sorbisch method.

Equipment and materials

A fine pencil
3 kistkas, 1 each fine, medium and thick *or* steel nib stuck into a pen holder
A heavy jar to hold the wax mixture
Drinking glass
Bowl of cold water
Candle stump or night light
Wax mixture of half beeswax to guarantee adherence and half stearin to guarantee fluidity
Paper towel or handkerchief
Newspapers
Absorbent cloth
Final varnish, or bacon rind

Note: The point of a fine pen nib or a funnel with a stopper may produce finer work than a kistkas because they can be handled like a pen.

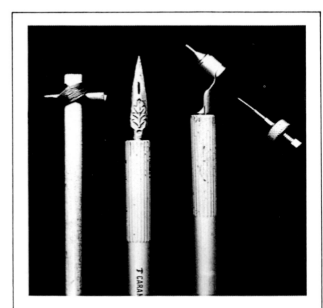

Tools for the pisankis method include a kistkas or pen-nib, or a funnel with a stopper.

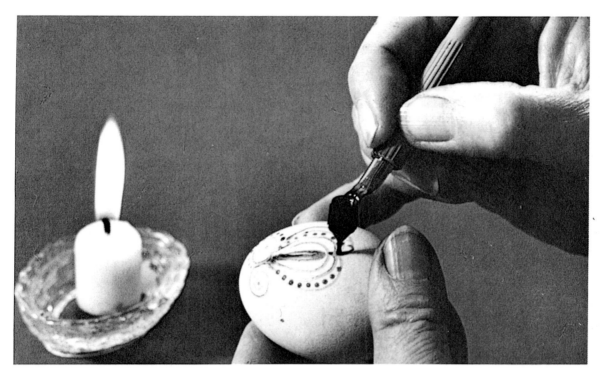

The wax will remain fluid in the heated funnel for a few minutes.
The funnel pen can be manipulated like a pencil.

Method

Heat the funnel of the kistkas near the candle flame. If you heat it over the flame soot is very quickly formed! Press a little piece of wax, the size of a pea, down into the funnel and allow it to melt. Test the liquid wax on a piece of newspaper to see if it is fluid.

Hold the kistkas at right angles on to the eggshell and allow the wax to flow out evenly and in clean lines.

Tip

The funnel should not be heated to excess or you may not be able to control the flow of the wax and it may drip on to the egg. If you have to scrape off any accidental wax stains, the shell will not take any more dye in that particular spot.

Kistkas

The writing implement of the kistkas becomes coated with wax and can easily catch alight. The flame may be blown out without too much difficulty.

If the writing tube is blocked, it can be cleaned with a fine needle when empty. If it is filled with hot wax, however, it may be gently but repeatedly knocked on to a piece of newspaper to release any solidified wax.

Pens

The nib is heated over the candle flame and then dripped into the pot containing the wax mixture. Hold the nib back over the flame for a second, then on to the egg to begin the design.

The beauty of this method is that you can control the thickness of the line by choosing a fine or thick nib. The other great advantage is that the wax does not begin to smoke.

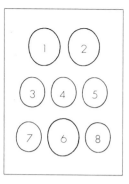

Batik designs, *opposite.*

1,2,3. Hen's egg, pisankis method. *Elisabeth Schlunegger.*
   4. Hen's egg, combined methods. *Erika Ineichen.*
   5. Hen's egg, pisankis method. *Paula Kunzli.*
   6. Hen's egg, sorbisch method. *Lenchen Hansel.*
   7. Hen's egg, combined methods, wax not melted away. *Auguste Mann.*
   8. Goose egg, pisankis method. *Paula Kunzli.*
   9. Hen's egg, pisankis method. *Paula Kunzli.*

Batik designs, *see page 62.*

1,2. Hen's egg, pisankis method. *Paula Kunzli.*
3–5. Hen's egg, sorbisch method. *Brigitte Raab.*
   6. Goose egg, pisankis method. *Heidi Haupt.*
7,8. Hen's eggs, sorbisch method. *Brigitte Raab.*

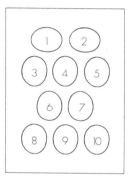

Batik designs, *see page 63.*

1–7. Pisankis method. *Ihor Kordink.*
8–10. Pisankis method. From the National Huzulen collection.

The British Protection
of Birds Act 1954
made the taking and selling of
wild birds' eggs illegal. It was updated
in 1982 in the Wildlife and Countryside Act.
This Act states that it is an offence
to take, sell, destroy or have
in one's possession any wild bird's egg.
It is not, however, an offence to own
old eggs collected during Victorian times,
provided that the age and the source of
the eggs can be substantiated.
But, however intrinsically valuable
an old collection is, it is now an offence to sell it
and you stand the risk of a heavy fine if you do.
Use only domestic or caged bird eggs.
The Control of Trade and Endangered Species
Enforcement Regulations 1985 states that birds'
eggs cannot be imported unless an import licence is
obtained, therefore you must check your source
very carefully before buying imported eggs.
Laws protecting wildlife universally
are complex and comprehensive and it is
wise to check with your
local Conservation Society before
choosing eggs for this craft.